Sing A Song Of Seasons

SING A SONG OF SEASONS

SING A SONG

OF

SEASONS

By
WILHELMINA SEEGMILLER
*Author of "Little Rhymes for Little Readers" and "Other Rhymes
for Little Readers"*

Illustrated by the Author

RAND McNALLY & COMPANY

CHICAGO   NEW YORK

The Rand-McNally Press
Chicago

Sing! Sing!

SING! Sing!
What shall I sing?
Of Winter, of Autumn,
Of Summer, of Spring.
Sing! Sing!

SPRING

SUMMER

AUTUMN

WINTER

Spring

The Spring will bid ▭—▭ ▭▱▭ Her flowers appear.

Spring Dreams

THOUGH pines and firs are weighted now
  So they can scarcely sing,
Though chill winds blow, and snowflakes
    whirl,
  I'm dreaming dreams of spring.

According to the calendar
  The winter days are done;
And soon the icicles will drip
  And snow melt in the sun.

The Spring will bid her flowers appear,
  And song of lark and thrush,
Of oriole and vireo,
  Will break the winter hush.

Though pines and firs are weighted now
  So they can scarcely sing,
Though chill winds blow, and snowflakes
    whirl,
  I'm dreaming dreams of spring.

13

Blow, Winds, Blow!

BLOW, winds, blow!
    What if the trees are bare,
There's the flurry of snow, the pond locked,
    And the frost still in the air.

Sing, trees, sing!
    'Way up on the topmost bough;
Where the twigs make lace on the tree crowns,
    The buds are swelling now.

And soon, oh, soon!
    Will the wingéd keys alight,
And the tassels swing in the breezes
    And take to airy flight.

For now, oh, now!
    The sap is running high,
And the days of song and blossom
    Are swiftly drawing nigh.

Good-by to Winter

GOOD-BY, good-by to Winter,
  For Winter's almost done,
And now the snow is melting
  In patches in the sun.

The Spring has sent her vanguards,
  The pussy-willows gray,
So up the land she's marching
  Dum, dum, de-dum, de, da!

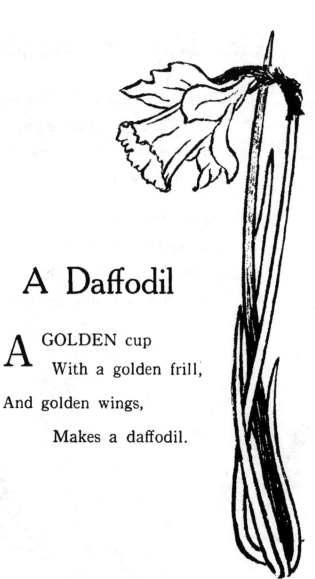

A Daffodil

A GOLDEN cup
  With a golden frill,
And golden wings,
  Makes a daffodil.

Sunshiny Showers

" A SUNSHINY shower
     Won't last half an hour,"
So the proverbs say;
When the sun takes pains
To shine when it rains,
We lose little time from play.

"The April showers
Bring the May-time flowers,"
So the wise ones say;
But the sunshiny showers
Bring us springtime flowers
Before the first of May.

A sunshiny shower,
An April flower,
A rainbow in the sky,
And a bird to sing,
"Spring, Spring, Spring, Spring!"
Oh, who is so gay as I?

17

The Spring has Come

OH, the Winter's gone away, and the
Spring's in green array,
And the little brook so happy is, it gurgles
night and day.

Now with a cheery song, Robin Redbreast
hops along,
Finding worms and bugs, and bugs and
worms and bugs the whole day long.

There are babies in the nest, in the silver
maple's crest;
So hungry they, the livelong day, that Robin
has no rest.

When a wandering breeze comes by, pink-
    flushed apple petals fly
And drift to orchard paths, and there like
    snowdrifts lie.

Every morning shows anew sparkling drops
    of silver dew
That glint, and gleam, and scintillate, until
    up in the blue

The sun smiles down at them, when each
    glinting, gleaming gem
Evaporates from grassy blade, and bud,
    and flower, and stem.

Oh, the Winter's gone away, and the happy
    children play;
They hop, and skip, and dance, and sing
    for merriness in May.

Spring

BONNY are the hillsides
　　And the flowering dells;
Bonny are the moorlands
　　And the reaching fells;

Bonny are the hedgerows;
　　And merry song-birds sing,
'Mid the bonny blooming,
　　"Spring! Spring! Spring!"

May Time

MAY time, gay time!
  Away! Away! 'T is play time!
  In and out the rushes,
  Beneath the alder bushes,
  The laughing water rushes;
  From throats of larks and thrushes
  The glad song bursts and gushes;
  The apple orchard blushes,
  The thorn to rose-pink flushes.
May time, gay time!
Away! Away! 'T is play time!
'T is May! 'T is May! Away! Away!
      Away!

A Flower Riddle

WHAT happy little flower,
  Any May-time day or hour,
Like a yellow disk of gold may be
  found, found, found?

Oh, it turns to silver gray,
And the silver blows away;
Then no flower at all is seen on the
  ground, ground, ground.

Humming Bee

HUMMING bee,
  Hum songs to me.
Hum about the trees that look
At themselves down in the brook,
While the brook runs babblingly,
Singing, singing to the sea.

Hum about the elves that sup
From a last year's acorn cup,
While new dishes growing show,
Where the oak-tree branches blow.

Hum about the sparkling lights
That the fireflies light o' nights,
Making turn and turn about,
Light and dark, till stars go out.
    Humming bee,
    Hum songs to me.

Possessions

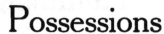

THE pines have long needles,
  The maples have keys,
The ash trees have paddles
  That drift in the breeze;

The poplars have tassels
  To swing in the parks,
And down in the dingles
  Ferns make question marks

Reflections

I LOVE the rain-wet pavements;
    They double all the trees,—
The oaks, the poplars, elms,
    The pines, and hickories.

And when the clouds go sailing,
    Go sailing swiftly by,
You see them sailing lowly,
    And see them sailing high.

And when a dove or sparrow
    Goes flying to the blue,
You watch it flying upward,
    And flying downward too.

And if by happy fortune
    A friend you chance to meet,
Like tree, and cloud, and sparrow,
    He's doubled on the street.

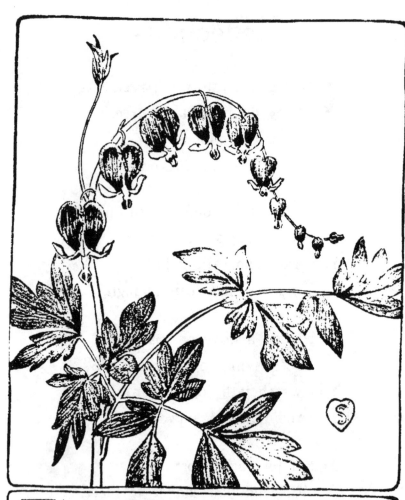

The pink Dicentra is a plant ♡♡
& With hearts of many sizes.

Hearts

THE pink Dicentra is a plant
  With hearts of many sizes,
For hearts quite large and little too,
  The pink Dicentra prizes.

And so she strings from large to small,
  Each pretty heart suspended,
Till with a very tiny heart
  The chain of hearts is ended.

A Happy Word

THIS morn I heard a happy word.
　　'Twas warbled in a tree,
And sung by many birds in turn,
　　Until it made a glee.

'Twas caught up by a tuneful brook
　　That with a meter free
Took it singing, singing on,
　　In greeting to the sea.

The word! The word! And what was it?
　　Ah, that I do not know;
I only know it happy was,
　　My heart went singing so.　　　·

Summer

One's turned back its petals curly,
And two buds will blossom surely.

One Sweet Lily

EVERY morn, when one arises,
  In the garden are surprises,
For strange things can happen nightly
In a place where flowers bloom brightly.

'Mid its green leaves, tall and stately,
One sweet lily has blown lately,
One's turned back its petals curly,
And two buds will blossom surely.

Springtime brought a daffodilly,
Summer has a garden lily;
Tell me how, by rime or reason,
Each plant knows its blooming season.

Wishing

I WISH I were a daisy, a daisy, a daisy,
I wish I were a daisy, with a golden eye
bright,
Nodding in the grasses;
The happy lads and lasses
A-Juning in the meadow would spy me with
delight.

I wish I were a pink rose, a pink rose,
a pink rose,
A sweet brier pink rose, blooming on a spray;
The butterflies would kiss me,
The honeybees would miss me,
When pink petals loosening would flutter
light away.

I wish I were a sparrow, a sparrow, a sparrow,
A sweet song sparrow singing in a tree;
My throat I'd swell with pleasure,
And without stint or measure
I'd carol forth my rapture in glad song free.

But I may love the daisy, the daisy, the daisy,
I may love the daisy with its golden eye,
And I may love and share in
The joy of rose and birdkin,
And so I wish for nothing, nothing, noth-
ing, I.

Robin

ROBIN rises early,
At the dawn of day.
Robin rises early;
And what does Robin say?

Robin calls, "Good morning!
Wake, and hasten up!
Dewy diamonds glisten
In each flower cup!

"Grasses all are beaded,
Buds of yesterday
Now are open roses,
Nodding every way."

33

Tree Windows

WONDROUS things you often see
Through the windows of a tree,—
Steeples pointing to the sky,
Happy birds a-flying by,
Housetops, and tall chimneys, too,
And white clouds high in the blue.

Red, Blue, and Gold

WHAT is red, red, red?
  A rose by the garden wall—
A dear little rose and a sweet little rose
That grows on a rose tree tall.

What is blue, blue, blue?
The sky on a summer day;
And the pretty brook that singing goes,
Is blue as it runs on its way.

And what is gold, gold, gold?
The sun that rides on high,
The daisy's eye in the meadow,
And the wings of a butterfly.

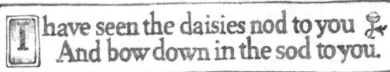
I have seen the daisies nod to you
And bow down in the sod to you.

O Singing Wind

I HAVE seen the daisies nod to you,
And bow down in the sod to you,
    O Singing Wind!
Do they whisper, "Come and play,"
        to you?
Please tell me what they say to you,
    O Singing Wind!

I have seen great white clouds sail for
        you,
And little white clouds trail for you,
    O Singing Wind!
The blue sky is a sea for you,
Where cloud ships all sail free for you,
    O Singing Wind!

I have seen the tree leaves kiss for you,
And dance in joy and bliss for you,
    O Singing Wind!
And when they say "Good-by" to you, .
I've heard them gently sigh for you,
    O Singing Wind!

My Lady's Garden

HOW does my lady's garden
    grow,
  Garden grow, garden grow,
How does my lady's garden grow,
  All of a summer morning?

Pinks and phlox and roses blow,
  Roses blow, roses blow,
Pinks and phlox and roses blow,
  All of a summer morning.

Lily bells the bees beguile,
  Bees beguile, bees beguile
Lily bells the bees beguile,
  All of a summer morning.

Happy pansies smile and smile,
  Smile and smile, smile and
    smile,
Happy pansies smile and smile,
  All of a summer morning.

38

Why Not?

WHY may not I love the pansies,
  And why may not pansies love me?
The pansies are smiling and happy,
And I am as gay as can be.

Why may not I love rosemary,
And why may not rosemary love me?
We both love the nook in the garden
By the side of the seckel pear tree.

And why may not I love the lilies,
And why may not lilies love me?
They furnish sweet nectar for honey,
And I love the hum of the bee.

Lady Wind

AT night, when my Lady Wind comes by,
  She says, "Oh, sing for me, trees!"
And they sing "Oo-oo! Oo-oo-oo!"
  When she fans with her lullaby
  breeze.

"Oo-oo-oo! Oo-oo-oo!"
  Then she rocks the birds in their
  nests,
While the little leaves join in the cradle
  song
  From the trunks to the tall tree
  crests.

"Oo-oo-oo! Oo-oo-oo!"
  And the stars look down to see
The sleeping birds in their rocking nests,
  Lady Wind, and a singing tree.

Butterfly

BUTTERFLY,
How I try,
As you hie,
To draw nigh;

But you go,
Swift, then slow,
To and fro;
And I know

I may run,
Just for fun,
In the sun,
Till day's done.

Snail, Snail

SNAIL, Snail, you are always at home,
Snail, Snail, where 'er you may roam,
Snail, Snail, for you carry about,
Snail, Snail, your whole house on your route.

Ladybird

DEAR Ladybird, in England
  They call you "Burnie Bee";
The children there say, "Bless you,
  When will you wedding be?"

But here we always tease you;
  We bid you hasten home,
And tell you of your house afire,
  Whene'er you chance to roam.

A bird on a lacey spray —◄—◄—◄—◄
Makes a bird on a spray in shadow.

Shadow Pictures

ONE beauty makes another.
   A happy, blooming rose
Makes a shadow rose beside it,
   That sways when the sweet air blows.

The meadow grass and daisies
   By the pathway may be found,
Whene'er the golden sun shines,
   Making pictures on the ground.

And sometimes, teeter-totter,
   A bird on a lacy spray
Makes a bird on a spray in shadow;
   I saw one yesterday.

Awake!

A ROSE flush bathes the morning skies,
      Awake!
The lark sings as it heavenward flies,
      "Daybreak!"
Soft tremors through the grasses run,
And sleepy flowers, one by one,
Lift heads in greeting to Lord Sun.
      Awake!

And now the sun resplendent rides,
      Awake!
He calls to hills and valleys wide,
      "Daybreak!"
The dew-gem's glistening on the rose,
The lily does her heart disclose,
O'er all the earth glad sunshine flows.
      Awake!

Twink! Twink!

TWINK, twink, twink, twink,
  Twinkity, twinkity, twink!
The fireflies light their lanterns,
  Then put them out in a wink.

Twink, twink, twink, twink,
  They light their lights once more,
Then twinkity, twinkity, twink, twink,
  They put them out as before.

Twink, twink, twink, twink,
  I would draw you a light or two,
But I have no golden pencil;
  With a black it is hard to do.

Weeds

THE weeds are very
    Beautiful
When gentle breezes
    Blow them,
And golden sunshine
    Kisses them;
I'm getting now to
    Know them.

The ragweed, bindweed,
    Milkweed, dock,
The velvet weed, and
    Purslane,
Stramonium, catnip,
    Shepherd's purse,
Teasel, poke,
    And vervain.

The weeds are happy
    In their life
As plants in garden
    Closes,
And dear to butterfly
    And bee
As mignonette
    And roses.

Garden Fairies

THE garden's full of fairies;
　　They have a happy time.
Up, up the strings of glories,
　　They climb, and climb, and climb.

And then by ones and couples,
　　And three, and four, and five,
As if the grass were water,
　　They gayly dip and dive.

They climb the stalks of roses,
　　And hide in hollyhocks;
They play tag 'round the larkspur,
　　And teeter on the phlox.

The garden's full of fairies;
　　They dance and sing and cheer.
But when you go to the garden,
　　They all just disappear.

If

IF I were a gnome in a forest home
  Where the trees grow thick and tall;
If I were a naiad, in the watery shade
  Of a tumbling waterfall;
If I were a fairy, with a dwelling airy
  In a ferny, flowery dell;
Or a shining mermaid, in a salt-sea glade
  Or a deep-down ocean dell;
If ifs could come true, oh, I know, don't
    you,
  That we'd laugh and leap for joy?
But the gnome and naiad airy, and the
    mermaid, and the fairy
  Might like to be a girl or boy.

Autumn

The sumach has its garnets, ——
—— Rose hips to corals turn.

Autumn Jewels

ALL up the autumn hillsides,
    And down the valley ways,
And by the singing rivers,
    The jewels of autumn blaze.

The sumach has its garnets,
    Rose hips to corals turn;
On mountain ash and alder
    Blood red the rubies burn.

And beads are on the linden,
    And beads are on the thorn,
And beads the brier and woodbine
    And trailing grape adorn.

With lapis, sard, and jasper,
    With amethyst and jade,
The trees and shrubs and vinings
    Of autumn are arrayed.

Cucumber Vines

THE vines of the cucumber
  Have blossoms golden bright;
They bloom in starry splendor,
Till frost puts out their light.

I like the starry blossoms,
I like cucumbers, too;
I like cucumber pickles
When autumn days are through.

Fall Gardens

THE gardens are amazing,
The flowers are burning,
blazing—
Nasturtiums gay are growing,
And salvias red are blowing;
The marigolds are flaming,
The dahlias' notice claiming;
Of color spread
In the zinnia bed
Who'd undertake the naming?

The flowers in masses tumble,
The bees go rumble, bumble;
The morning-glory vining
Is twining, twining, twining;
'Way up to second stories
Are glories, glories, glories,
That gladly blow,
Ere comes the snow,
Ere comes the fall frost hoary.

And each stem's crest makes a bird's nest
When its white blooming ends. ⁂.

The Lace of Queen Anne

L IGHT and airy
  As a fairy,
Sprung in leafage of green
  On the highway
  And the byway,
The queen's lace is seen,

  . To the hillside
  And the rillside
Its beauty it lends,
  And each stem's crest
  Makes a bird's nest
When its white blooming ends.

A Little Seed

THERE was a little seed;
It was very small, indeed,
But it made a little plant, and it grew,
grew, grew;
The plant became a vine,
It had blossoms eighty-nine.
While the tale is very strange, it is true,
true, true.

Jolly October

THE pears now are mellow,
  The pumpkins are yellow,
Ripe chestnuts are falling,
The late birds are calling,
To gold, leaves are turning,
Great bonfires are burning,
The pecker is drumming,
The bees still go humming,
The sunshine comes streaming—
Ah, can folk be dreaming?
Why say they you're sober,
You jolly October?

Apple Fragrance

HAD I a hundred noses
   I'd use them, every one,
To smell the golden apples
When they're kissed by the autumn sun.

A Windfall

UPON the tree s high, rounded crest
  The golden apples grow the best,
For there the sun first kisses them,
And makes each one a blushing gem.

As I can't reach high in the tree,
The good wind loosens fruit for me;
And in the mornings oft I find,
The wind's been very, very kind.

Most autumn days, when breakfast's done,
I run out in the golden sun,
And visit some big apple tree
To find what the wind has done for me.

Milkweed Seeds

A S white as milk,
   As soft as silk,
And hundreds close together;
They sail away,
On an autumn day,
When windy is the weather.

The Rill

THE clouds sail swift
And the clouds sail high,
As they pass o'er the red-gold hill;
And the leaves drop red,
And the leaves drop gold,
And they run with the running rill.

And the rill sings high
And the rill sings low,
Of the ships on the distant sea,
Where the tide runs in,
And the tide runs out,
And the gull soars high and free.

And I would laugh,
And I would run,
With the rill to the shining sea;
But if I were there,
They would miss me here,—
The reeds, and the willow tree.

Acorns

ANY acorn in its cup
   May spread branches out and up;
Any acorn on the tree
May some day a king oak be.

Beechnuts

DID you gather beechnuts
 When you were a girl?
Oh, when I gather beechnuts
 I'm happy as an earl.

Beech burrs are rough and pricky,
 But when there comes a frost
They open, and their treasures
 Upon the breeze are tossed.

When nuts are scattered broadcast,
 And lying brown and thick,
I sit right down among them
 And pick, and pick, and pick.

The leaves above are golden,
 The leaves beneath are brown,
And beechnuts from above me
 Drop, drop, drop down.

The Windy Man

HINKITY, winkity, pinkity, pan!
How do you like the Windy Man?
"Wo-oo-oo!" he sings as he goes,
And down from the trees the leaves he blows.

The nuts go pittery, pittery, pat,
The reeds and the rushes bow down flat,
The ripples run, and they race to shore,
When the Windy Man strides o'er the water
floor.

Hinkity, winkity, pinkity, pan!
How do you like the Windy Man?
"Wo-oo-oo!" he sings as he goes,
And everything slams, and bangs, and blows.

Hinkity, winkity, pinkity, pan!
How do you like the Windy Man?

Flying South

THE birds go flying, flying by
    Above the fir-tree steeple,
And soon they'll sing their happy
        songs,
    'Tis said, for southern people.

The bees have left the garden ways;
    There's no buzz of arriving;
They've stored their honey for the
        year
    And now, I guess, they're hiving.

And soon, oh, soon, when leaves are
        blown
    And snow lies all a-glitter,
We shall not have a song or hum,
    But just the sparrow's twitter.

I'm glad the sparrow stays behind,
    With barren eaves contented;
If he should southward go, I'm sure
    He'd sorely be lamented.

November

NOVEMBER is earth's resting time;
    The corn is bound in shocks;
And overhead late-lingering birds
    To new climes fly in flocks;
The calm pools left by autumn rains
    Are mirrors for the sky,
And in their cool, sweet restfulness
    The bare tree branches lie.

Winter

Do all the birds to the southlands go?
No! No! O, no! ▫▪▭▪▪ ▪▪▭▭▪▫

Winter Birds

Do all the birds
  To the southlands go?
    No!
    No!
    Oh, no!
    Chickadee,
    Sparrow,
    Bunting,
    Crow
Care not a whit
When the wild winds blow.
  They care not a whit,
  They're sad not a bit,
  They think naught of it,
When the wild winds blow.

December

DECEMBER trees
  Show traceries
Clear cut against the sky;
    Dead leaves are guests
    In empty nests,
Or 'neath snow carpets lie;
    But still the green
    Of hemlock's seen,
And anthems still are mine,
    Of pointed fir,
    And juniper,
Of balsam, spruce, and pine.

Snow

SOFT flakes of snow
   Like feathers blow,
Then settle languidly
   On every twig,
   And every sprig,
Till vine, and shrub, and tree
   Are decked in white,
   And in sunlight
The spangles sparklingly
   Smile at the sun,
   Till every one
A diamond seems to be.

Chickadee

NOW the tall trees shake and shiver;
On the pond, and lake, and river
Winter's laid an icy finger.
Some brave birds have dared to linger,
And they sing quite cheerily,
"Chick-a-dee-dee, chick-a-dee,
Chick-a-dee-dee-dee!
Dee-dee
Dee-dee
Chick-a-dee,
Chick-a-dee-dee-dee!"

Christmas Trees

WHAT sings the breeze
　　To the wee fir trees?
"O little trees, grow high,
　　For far away,
　　On a Christmas day,
They may need you, by and by."

　　And the golden sun
　　On every one
Shines warm, and kind, and bright,
　　And tells each tree
　　It may one day be
Aglow with candle light.

　　And the moon above
　　Shines down in love,
And the stars sing night by night:
　　"Peace, good will to men!
　　Oh, grow, and then
You may be crowned by a Christ star
　　bright."

75

Green Things Growing

WINTER has its green things growing;
Pines care not for frost or snowing,
Beautiful is arbor vitæ.
Balsam, fir, and spruce make quite a
Posy when white snow is gleaming;
When of Christmas time we're dreaming,
Winter gives us berries jolly,
Mistletoe, and crimson holly.

Thick Fur and Feather

THICK fur and feather
　　Help in cold weather
The squirrel and chickadee-dee;
　　The foxes and rabbits
　　Just thicken their habits
When winds from the northlands blow
　　　　free.

　　Such simplicity!
　　How fine it must be,
As the new seasons begin,
　　To suit fur or feather
　　To warm or cold weather,
By changing to thick or to thin.

Snow Crystals

HOW I love to see them blow,
Airy crystals of the snow!
Each one like a blossom fair
Dropping from the upper air.

And when snowy flakes you pass
'Neath a magnifying glass,
You can see the airy lines
Of the fairylike designs.

When Jack Frost Paints
the Windowpane

THE ferns grow in the woodland dells,
    The streams wind through the moors
      and fells,
The forests lift tree-columns high,
And leafy crests wave 'gainst the sky
On mountain side and spreading plain,—
When Jack Frost paints the windowpane.

The castles rise with turrets tall,
And battlement, and moat, and wall,
As fair as castles ever seen
As home of prince, or king, or queen
Who dwell in palace halls in Spain,—
When Jack Frost paints the windowpane.

Sometimes you view the rolling sea,
When waves roll high and winds blow free,
With stately ships with anchor cast,
Or sails full spread before the blast;
Oh, many things are pictured plain,—
When Jack Frost paints the windowpane.

When a nest you find, do you know what kind
Of little bird loved it best? ◦ ◦◦◦ ◦

Winter Nests

YOU oft may see, in a winter tree,
  A woven basket nest.
When a nest you find, do you know what
      kind
  Of little bird loved it best?

Do you know the song that, the whole day
      long,
  Was caroled glad and free,
While a brooding breast kept warm in the
      nest
  Eggs one and two and three?

Oh, eggs take wing to soar and to sing,
  And little birds leave the nest;
When a nest you find, do you know what
      kind
  Of little bird loved it best?

The New Moon

THE new moon is a slight moon,
  Of sheeny, shiny gold,
But the moon will be a round moon
  When the little moon grows old.

A ring we now see faintly;
  A round moon there will be;
Then I'll smile up at the moon man,
  And he'll smile down at me.

The Wish Star

THE twinking, winking wish star,
    On a winter's night,
The first one in the gloaming
    To light its little light,
Hears many, many wishes
    Of many, many kinds.
And sometimes, too, the wishes
    The twinking wish star finds
So very contradictory
    They can't all granted be.
When folks wish things just opposite,
    The wish star thinks, "Dear me!"

The Year

THE year is a circle.
  One, two, three, and four
The seasons that make it,
And o'er, o'er, and o'er
Each follows another.
So therefore 't is plain
That when winter's ending,
Spring's coming again.

DAISY, daisy, tell to me,
  When I'm grown what shall I be?
Rich man, poor man, beggar man,—*thief?*
Oh, that passes all belief!

Daisy, daisy, I'll be good,
Just as every grown-up should,
Always do the thing I ought!
I will—sometimes—like as not!

From *Little Rhymes for Little Readers,* by Wilhelmina Seegmiller
With illustrations by Ruth Mary Hallock
Price, $1.00

RAND McNALLY & COMPANY

OTHER BOOKS BY WILHELMINA SEEGMILLER

REDBREAST IN THE CHERRY TREE

REDBREAST, in the cherry tree,
  Robin red, it seems to me
That you love the cherries so
You eat all a tree can grow.
You love cherries, so do I.
Please leave some for cherry pie!

From *Other Rhymes for Little Readers,*
by Wilhelmina Seegmiller
With illustrations by Ruth M. Hallock.
Price, $1.25

RAND McNALLY & COMPANY

CPSIA information can be obtained
at www.ICGtesting.com
Printed in the USA
LVHW081430110621
690001LV00002B/102